the GREATEST Reggae collection EVER!

CW00742401

Compiled by Miranda Steel
Cover Design: London Advertising Partnership
Published 1999

IMP
International MUSIC Publications

© International Music Publications Limited
Griffin House 161 Hammersmith Road London W6 8BS England

Baby Come Back

Words and Music by
EDDY GRANT

Warner/Chappell Music Ltd, London W6 8BS

4

2. There ain't no use in you crying
   'Cause I'm more hurt than you
   I should have not been a flirting
   But now my love is true,
   Ooh, ooh, ooh, yeah.

3. Come back baby don't you leave me
   Baby baby please don't go
   Oh won't you give me a second chance
   Baby I love you so,
   Oh, oh, oh, yeah.

Dreadlock Holiday

Words and Music by
ERIC STEWART and **GRAHAM GOULDMAN**

6

Everything I Own

Words and Music by
DAVID GATES

You shel-tered me _ from harm,

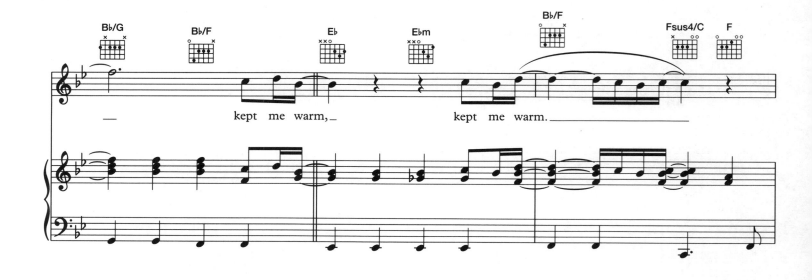

kept me warm, _ kept me warm. _

You gave my life _ to me, _ set me free, _ set me free. _

It Hurts So Good

Words and Music by
PHILLIP MITCHELL

I Don't Wanna Dance

Words and Music by
EDDY GRANT

The Israelites

Words and Music by
DESMOND DACRES and **LESLIE KONG**

Moderately slow

Get up in the morn-ing, slav-ing for bread,__ sir, so that ev-er-y mouth__

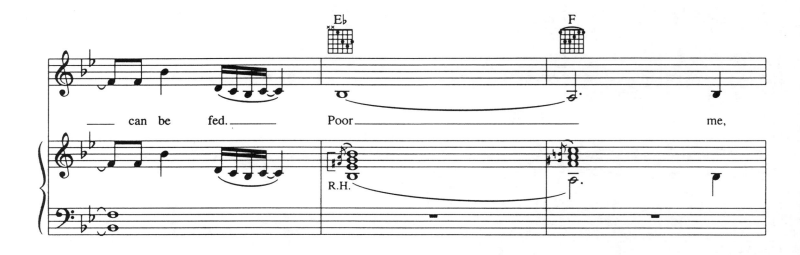

__ can be fed.__ Poor_____ me,

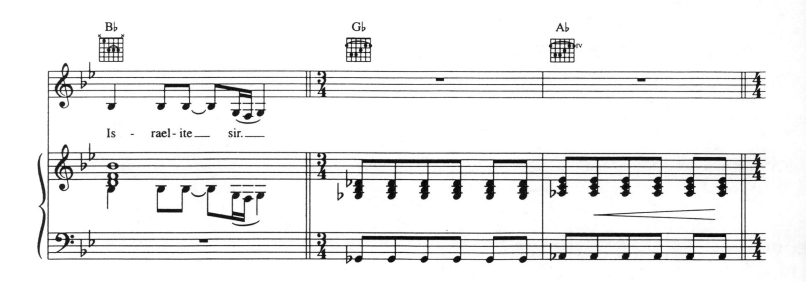

Is - rael-ite__ sir.__

I'm In The Mood For Love

Words and Music by
JIMMY McHUGH and DOROTHY FIELDS

Kingston Town

Words and Music by
CLANCY ECCLES

No Woman No Cry

Words and Music by
VINCENT FORD and **BOB MARLEY**

meet, good friends we have_ oh good friends we've lost
night, then we would cook corn meal por - ridge,
Am F C G Am F
a-long the way___ in this great fu - ture,
of which I'll share with you___ ooh___ my feet is my
C G Am F C G
you can't for - get your past___ So dry your tears___ I
on - ly car - riage___ So I've got to push on
Am F C G
1 2
say. And through. But while I'm gone I mean,
Am F Am F G

Shine

Words and Music by
JOSEPH CANG, ANGUS GAYE, DENNIS ROBERTSON,
BRINSLEY FORD and RICK WAKEMAN

- ture, spread-ing your light_____ wher-ev-er you are._____

✦ *CODA*

Shine, shine like a star,____ shin-ing so bright__ like the star that you are._

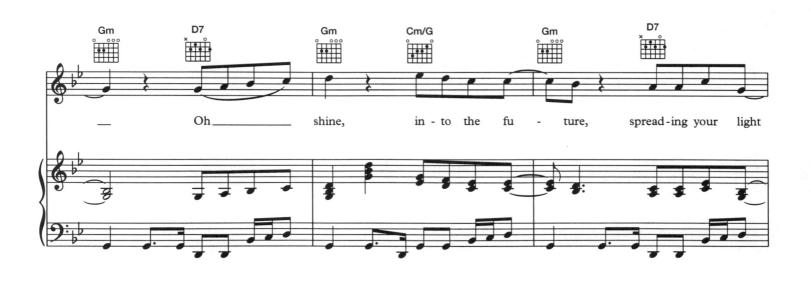

__ Oh_____ shine, in - to the fu - ture, spread-ing your light

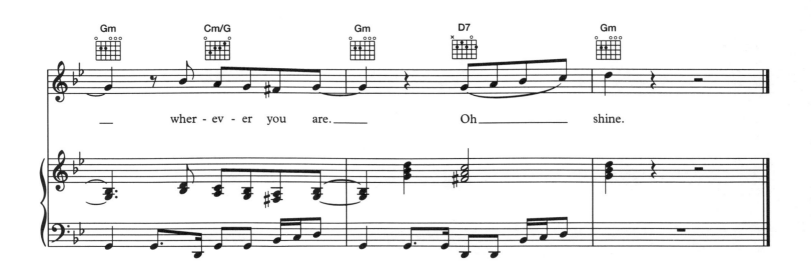

__ wher - ev - er you are.____ Oh_____ shine.

We've Got A Good Thing Going

Words and Music by
FREDDIE PERREN, ALPHONSO MIZELL,
DENNIS LUSSIER and BERRY GORDY

48

You Don't Love Me (No No No)

Words and Music by
WILLIE COBBS

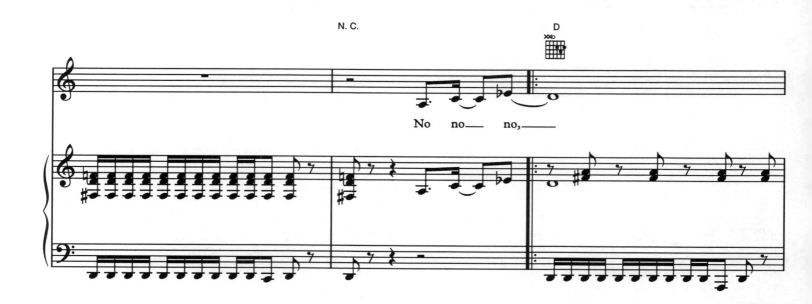

peo - ple: scene, tell the, tell the, tell the peo - ple, tell the peo - ple.
—— boy,——

'cause you left—— me———— ba - by,————————
'cause if you ask—— me———— ba - by,————————

and I got no place to go—— now, tell the peo - ple: scene,
I'll get on my knees and pray—— boy, tell the peo - ple:

tell the peo-ple: scene.

No no— no,

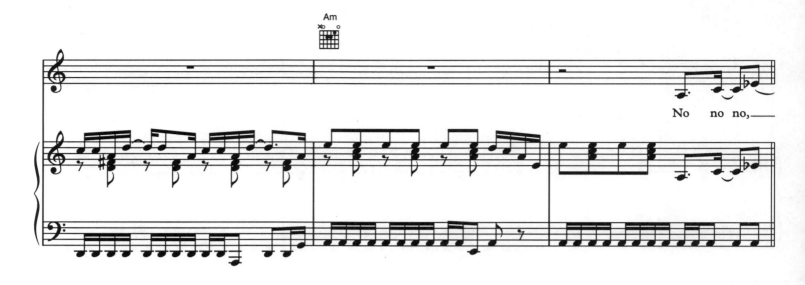

No no no,___

you don't love me, and I___ know
you don't love me, yes I___ know

___ now.___

No no___ no,

___ now.___

repeat ad lib. to fade

repeat ad lib. to fade

A Message To You Rudy

Reggae

Words and Music by
ROBERT THOMPSON

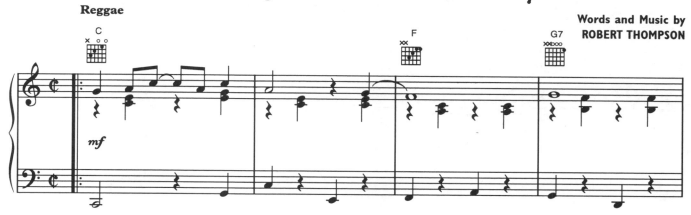

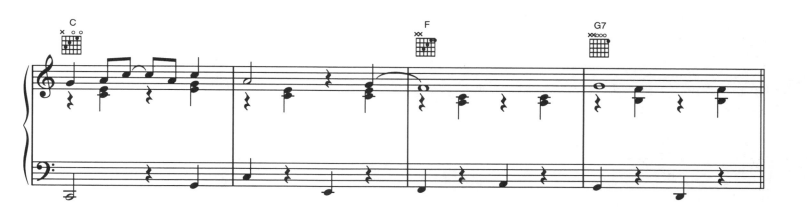

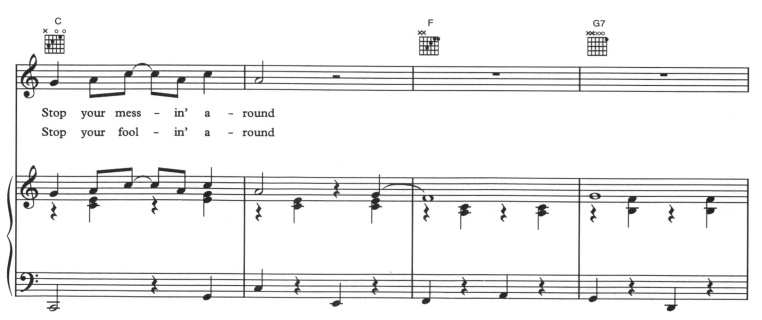

Stop your mess – in' a – round
Stop your fool – in' a – round

bet - ter   think_ of your fu - ture
time you   straight - ened right   out

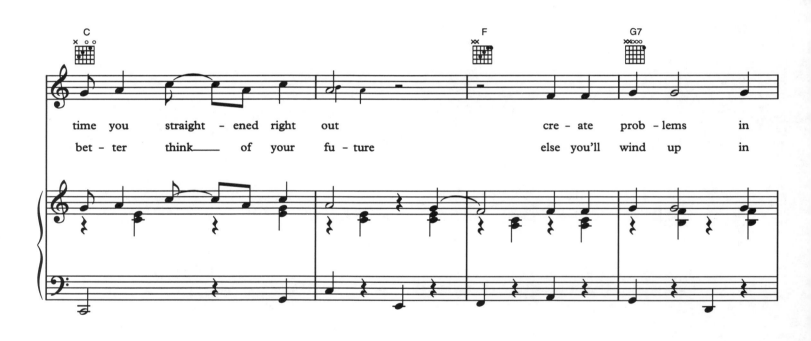

time you   straight - ened right   out   cre - ate   prob - lems   in
bet - ter   think_ of your   fu - ture   else you'll   wind up   in

town. }
jail. }   Ru - -

Printed in England
The Panda Group · Haverhill · Suffolk · 7/99

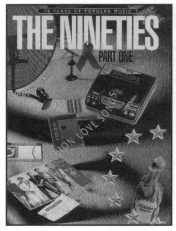
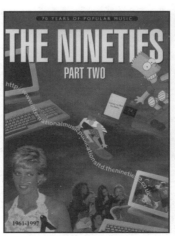